# SIMPLY ABRAHAM

## MARZIEH GOLBAR

**BALBOA**
PRESS
A DIVISION OF HAY HOUSE

Balboa Press books may be ordered through booksellers or by contacting:

Balboa Press
A Division of Hay House
1663 Liberty Drive
Bloomington, IN 47403
www.balboapress.com
1 (877) 407-4847

Print information available on the last page.

ISBN: 978-1-5043-9597-7 (sc)
ISBN: 978-1-5043-9598-4 (e)

Balboa Press rev. date: 07/02/2018

*Y*ou have heard this many times, the "present moment". When this concept was introduced to me for the first time, I had difficulty making a distinction between past, present, and, future at a given moment because I was living under strong influence of my past and the illusion of what was yet to come. Practically, I had no idea what present moment may have meant or be. As I thought more about it, I had to practice keeping my thoughts where I wanted to go or what I intended to do, and keep focus on whatever was pertaining to my daily activities including work. Eventually and regrettably, I realized that, a big chunk of my "present moments" had been nothing but operating on autopilot, missing out on the most important part of my day, the "now".

That's right. Stop thinking about the past tense and do not be afraid of "what is next". Unlearn what you have learned in school. Take "time" out of the grammar context very much like taking a picture out of its frame and feel the freedom of NOW. If this sounds difficult, do it Abraham's way:

"There is nothing for you to go back and live over, or fix, or feel regret about now. Every part of your life has unfolded just right. And so—now—knowing all that you know from where you now stand, now what do you want? The answers are now coming forth to you. Go forth in joy, and get on with it."

One of the big reasons for missing out on "now" is the regret, resentment, or any negative emotion associated with the past and the fear of what we can't control; the future events. Most of us go through the pain and discomfort of being pulled in two opposite directions; and the fact that we must perform our daily routine from day to day, wishing life was easier or keeping our fingers crossed the economics or other trends make a turn in our favor not knowing in order to have a desirable future it is taking charge of our present NOT controlling the future that makes a enormous difference regardless what had happened in the past.

At first, in search of better ways for living, I encountered Abraham's philosophy, which seemed too simplistic or too good to be true. However, with a little patience and practice I realized that, actually, it works and there is a lot more to it. The concept of "propagation of uncertainty" in analytical chemistry helped me understand why this works the way it does.

In very simple term, suppose you are to use a series of related and stepwise formulas to calculate some variable.

An extremely small mistake in calculations at step one can grow into a statistically significant error at the end. Small negative thoughts can add and potentiate one another's effect. By the same mechanism, positive thoughts or good vibes add up. Try it. One small feel good thought at a time.

If you can't feel joy for whatever reason then take some "time off" even for a very short bit. This means thinking about nothing. Considering what our thoughts are made of ie. mostly worry, guilt, shame, doubt, anger, fear... and the fact that they occur almost effortlessly because we tend to think negatively as our lives are NOT always as we want or desire, thinking about nothing will be challenging for most of us including myself. The thing is, we can start from a 30 seconds at a time and continue practicing until we can sit down with a "quiet mind" for 5, 10, or 15 minutes. The advantage of this, when accomplished in full, is a lifetime benefit of ability to tune in to all good vibes of the universe. As much as one may argue with the benefit of a calm and clean mind you need to clear your busy head from all sorts of thoughts. Stay away from any sort of judgment as best as you can. What you keep saying or thinking becomes! Seriously.

> "You cannot continue to beat the drum of things that don't feel good when you beat them without filling your future experience full of things that don't feel good. At some point, there's going to be

a tipping point that's going to become a manifestation."

Abraham

Remember to use your emotions as your guideline. What are you feeling right now? Do you feel good? Are you bored, angry, disappointed, frustrated, ashamed, confused... what are you really feeling? Are you aware of your emotional state at this moment or at any given point in your daily life? Whatever you do make sure you do not get stuck in the negative rut.

Our clever friend Abraham has a very easy and practical way of getting out of such "rut". Something very true and always neglected and unrealized is how easily we get turned off and mislead by our own habits:

> "You have the ability to pivot under any and all conditions. But most of you are habitual in nature, and your patterns are so well entrenched..."

In order to understand this we need to understand the basics about our mind. In very simple term, we are under influence of our surrounding environment from the moment we are born. Every experience with our five senses is organized and structured by our brain. Abraham is referring to these structures as "patterns". Once these patterns are formed they will undergo changes, but only those changes that make them stronger and more prominent. This is because as we progress and grow, our

mind only accommodates inputs from the environment that agree with these patterns and filters out everything else.

Thus, what remains and keeps growing is what we stored and started with at a very young age. It becomes the "habit" which is so effortless to do or to be. The further we are through the stages of our life, the more time and effort it takes to change these patterns and unless we become aware of this process and deliberately take action, things will stay as they are.

That is not all the resistance one may face when changing unwanted patterns. In other words, human mind is not just a screen that keeps conflicting information out. Very much like a thermostat that puts the room temperature back where it was set originally, our mind puts us where we used to be every time we attempt to make a change in our thoughts and behavioural patterns. The good news is there is a way to deal with self-sabotage and bad habits:

"...at times the fastest path to the joy you seek is for you to take your pivot as you sleep. By reaching for good-feeling thoughts before you go to sleep..."

This is when we can bypass the conscious mind almost, effortlessly, and let our subconscious mind do the work for us.

"... and then experiencing the benefit of the quiet mind that occurs while you sleep—and then upon awakening, immediately turning to good-feeling thoughts—you can accomplish the ultimate *Pivoting* experience."

Having said all of the above, bare in mind that thoughts that work against us are not always frankly "negative". We are very aware and can differentiate good and bad thoughts, however; what we may not realize is "indifference" which in my opinion is another form of negativity that may be more destructive and discouraging to our lives.

A negative thought makes us feel bad and miserable which consequently can become our motivation to take action and finding a resolution. Indifference, on the contrary, will shut down our mental faculties as well as killing the drive to look for solutions and taking action.

# WHAT YOU SEEK, SEEKS YOU!

More over, what you seek you find more like it:

I remember the first time I went camping in Banff, I was concerned about Grizzly bears, cougars, and elks attacking camp grounds, especially bears (I had heard) were getting used to human activity approaching hikers campers, and tourists. Although the advisors at the visitor center reassured us that there had been no reports of bears in the area we were camping, my fear got restored after entering the park where I saw the bear-proof garbage cans!

Later on that evening, in my tent, I spent a difficult night in fear because I was able to hear animals growling, indistinct but still noticeable, and walking around my tent. Of course the next day, no one, including the other two people in my tent, had heard anything, it was only my ears; that had heard the wild life sounds because I was alert and as I was trying to sleep on and off to detect danger.

Those who slept peacefully that night did not look for contradictions to what the trip advisors had said upon entering the park. They did not become all ears to hear animals walking in he vicinity or snarling. In other words, they did not SEEK trouble. If this is true (which it is) then the same principle should apply to seeking positive feel good aspects of everything:

> "When you deliberately seek positive aspects of whatever you are giving your attention to, you, in a sense, tune your vibrational tuner to more positive aspects of everything."

Be ware of the science behind like attracts like. In organic chemistry the notorious rule of laboratory: Like dissolves like states that polar solvents dissolve ONLY polar solutes. For example; water, a polar solvent dissolves polar solutes such as table salt, sugar, alcohol, dishwashing detergents… because salt gets ionized to its polar constituents Sodium ($Na+$) and Chloride ($Cl-$) and the rest have polar molecules caused by the same type of oxygen-hydrogen covalent bonds as in the **water** molecule.

Similarly, a non-polar solvent dissolves non-polar solute. For example, benzoic acid is highly soluble in ethanol and reasonably high in chloroform, but insoluble in water. One simple example, as you may have encountered this in your kitchen, try to mix water (polar) with oil (non-polar) and see if the two layers will ever agree with each other. However, as different and disagreeable positive and negative thoughts are, we have freedom to adapt because

we are not simply polar or non-polar molecules, positive or negative thoughts, we are able to deliberately (and as Abraham puts it) "tune" ourselves to whichever we choose:

> "And, of course, you could tune yourself negatively as well. But as you are deliberately looking for positive aspects in yourself or in others, you will find more of *those* things: "The better it gets, the better it gets," for you get more and more of what you are thinking about—whether you want it or not."

This is definitely science. The force of gravity never stops operating at any given time or place. It pulls you down by 9.8 m/s$^2$ almost everywhere on the planet. Laws of attraction work exactly the same way. Be ware of your thoughts and do not miss a thing. Alignment with abundance does not occur when your mind is on autopilot (unless you have trained yourself to think abundance). Many of us have too many negative ideas regarding money. There is a difference between what we want and what we lack. Abraham explains this beautifully:

> **"The Subject of Money Is Really Two Subjects...**
> The subject of money is really two subjects: (1) money, plenty of money, and (2) absence of money, not nearly enough money...When you are feeling fear or discomfort ... you are speaking of the subject of not enough money... the first

9

statement brings money and the second
holds it away."

This concept was very hard for me to understand and differentiate. A strong desire for anything we want that is not yet in our possession or a very positive and vivid image of what we really want is ALWAYS associated with even stronger feeling of not enough money (or anything we desire), but it could also be a result of looking at all those goodies which we do not have right now and we FEAR that we may never achieve them or "how am I going to have that" and consequently we feel discomfort and disappointment although we have been focusing on our desire and the positive thought.

So, this is when one says, "I am thinking positive thoughts and keeping with my positive affirmations regarding wealth, abundance, love, and happiness, but I don't have any of those things I truly desire, or have not fully achieved what I want..." then this proceeds to the conclusion that affirmations don't work or laws of attraction don't really exist and eventually one gets back to the same rut as before living from day to day like a robot repeating the same year after another.

The fact is positive thoughts are not a single, all or none thing. Just take an inventory of your thoughts and beliefs and examine them for "purity". If you think of an expensive luxurious house and feel happy and secure you are in alignment with possessing one, you are on the right track. On the contrary, if you feel uncomfortable, disappointment, thinking how is this possible for me, I'm

never going to have this at the same time, … then your positive thought or image about such house has NOT been positive at all.

What you are doing here is summoning conflicting thoughts and emotions, which get stronger and stronger (because it is law, like attracts like), and all of this is happening in a matter of seconds, and what comes out of it is discouragement, disillusionment, disappointment, and a new destructive idea: "This is not going to work" which will most likely turn off the enthusiasm and drive for thinking positively or doing anything constructive for your life.

Be smart. Thoughts are like coins. They have two sides positive and negative. So do the emotions they elicit in us: good and bad. Think positive, but at the same time beware of your emotions and feelings. Don't let the need to know how control your fun with your good thoughts and imaginations. Be the one who flips the coin in your favour and KEEP it on the positive side.

It may take some while to understand that unless one edits the positive images, thoughts, and desires of the contrasting components that are associated with them, one might as well prepare to take a lifetime for achieving anything he or she so deeply desires.

# GO AHEAD GET FANCY! NOT JUST FOR MONEY, BUT FOR EVERYTHING YOUR HEART DESIRES.

Get into the habit of creating and directing your thoughts. Whatever is happening outside your head, good or bad, negative trends, unfavourable economical circumstances, family and friends disapprovals and discouragements, all and all is not your concern; just have fun with the process and select what you think about,

> "I Can Always Tell a Different Financial Abundance Story. . .
> What anyone else has or does not have has nothing to do with you. The only thing that affects your experience is the way you utilize the Non-Physical Energy with your thought."

The most important message here, in my opinion, is our ability to focus. Distractions such as what is happening

now, or the fact that "presently, this is my real life" with all the things I can't have or be is the major barrier we need to breakthrough in order to achieve our "wants" and things we would love to have. Just keeping the focus on the fairy tale story:

> "...Your abundance or lack of it in your experience has nothing to do with what anybody else is doing or having. It has only to do with your perspective. It has only to do with your offering of thought. If you want your fortunes to shift, you have to begin telling a different story.

And it becomes easier to accept and practice something really simple but hard to believe as things start to manifest. This is how it all started for me. It did sound like magic, making me smile and feeling wonderful, but it was absolutely science:

> "It Comes, Not by Magic But by Universal Law
> Start telling a better-feeling story about the things that are important to you. Do not write your story like a factual documentary, weighing all the pros and cons of your experience..."

I am not saying we must deny the reality. Not at all. I am saying we must put emphasise on our desires by focusing and deliberate thinking. We must understand one thing: what is happening presently is already in progress. It is

what it is and complaining about it is simply stating the obvious. We must use our words to say what we want instead of describing our present circumstances. It can be trying especially for "reality oriented" minds, ie majority of us. This is common sense, especially, for educated people who's thoughts are evidence and reason based. In experimental science, for example, the physical and chemical properties of all substances are known and tabulated for reference. They are as they are and cannot change. The magic, though, comes into play when we utilize these numbers and fixed properties to create what we ardently desire!

What is so hard to realize is; our life events and situations are not fixed numbers and we can change them or even use them to create something desirable IF we truly want to do so. It all depends on how DABLY we want something. Badly enough to think about it and enjoy speaking about it; constantly:

> "...but instead tell the uplifting, fanciful, magical story of the wonder of your own life and watch what happens. It will feel like magic as your life begins to transform right before yours eyes, but it is not by magic. It is by the power of the *Laws of the Universe* and your deliberate alignment with those *Laws*."

I must admit that this has been challenging for me. It has been odd and awkward thinking in the direction other than what I see or, presently, able to have. I still

14

find myself struggling with doubts, at times. It is easy to talk about and at the same time difficult to do. We are visual beings for the most part. We believe what we can see easily and effortlessly. This "magical story" is very different than the life one is living at present. Too far from "reality" for the conscious mind to "accept" all that beauty, comfort, luxury, love... however, what will work better is taking one step at a time. One thought at a time and capitalizing on small victories as opposed to the whole chain of events (that have not happened yet). Take a look at the results, however small, that you have achieved by far and get back on the track. Know that something must have worked right and in your favour. Thinking for and in the direction of your goals and desires is only a habit, nothing more or less. Just do it:

> "I'm Developing the Skill to Direct My Thoughts. . .
> The most valuable skill or talent that you could ever develop is that of directing your thoughts toward what you want... There is a tremendous skill in deliberately directing your own thoughts that will yield results that cannot be compared with results that mere action can provide."

Our emotional state and how we feel matter most. We are constantly and deeply influenced by our everyday life. Whether we are students or in work force already, we are bombarded by positive/negative comments, criticisms, do's and don'ts, fairness and unfairness, must and must not …how do we feel at the end of the day? What is happening inside our head? Which thoughts stay strong and take the hold the rest of our day? What kind of self -talk do we have? Are we still focused on what we desire? What are we attracting? Or according to Abraham, what is our "point of attraction"? I will talk about this more but let me tell you something really interesting first.

I remember several times my cousins and I were playing a make believe scenario of I, acting as a doctor, examining my cousin who was acting the patient and one of the kids imitated the siren of ambulance. My grand mother who was busy sewing something at the other side of the room immediately interrupted us and said "…No! it is wedding! It is a birthday party! Play happy games kids!! Years later when I got introduced to Abraham, I understood the clever woman's logic:

> "The Better My Story Gets the Better My Life Gets. . .
> Begin telling the story of your desire, and then add to it the details of the positive aspects that you can find that match those desires. And then embellish your positive expectation by speculating with your good-feeling *Wouldn't it be nice if . . . ?*"

I would put a little more emphasis on what I want and tell my good feeling story a little differently. For example, "what if I got an A in my calculations exam" or "what if I got the best deal on that nice car" and this should be without doubts or uncomfortable disappointing thoughts

of "I don't have it yet" or quietly and simultaneously thinking to myself "how is this going to happen?" The better story will remain just a story as long as the burden of contradictions is associated with it. If this is challenging, which makes sense because we are under constant domination of our conscious mind or "Ego", just keep at it regardless. Let these thoughts pop out and immediately focus on the better feeling thought and say, "yes, I know, but I choose this one!" When practiced repeatedly, the positive thoughts will become unanimous; no flaws, no doubts, or guilt, or shame just that which is purely desired and it will have to materialize in your life.

Here are more of the better feeling stories from Abraham, but you may create your own as well:

> "…examples.
> You can say things like: *Only good things come to me… I'll figure it out as I go along. …* Every time you tell your better-feeling story, you will feel better and the details of your life will improve. The better it gets, the better it gets."

# WORRYING

Back to the grandma's story, I do not remember ever being allowed to talk or act negatively in her presence. She would immediately correct and rephrase my words if I made any remarks of being unhappy, crying, or having a bad luck either regarding myself, or my family members. She would not just tell me not to worry; she would ask me to think happy thoughts, laughing thoughts, and to speak good words. She told me the story of the bird named "Amen" that was always flying in the skies and if it flew over ones house whatever the people in that house have been talking about would become a reality.

Sounds like cliché but it is common practice in our daily lives. We say or hear this almost every day or several times a day, "I am worried about…" or "I am concerned about…" or "What if…" etc. I just can't help but remembering the lesson I learned years and years ago and just love the way Abraham puts it:

> "Worrying is using your imagination to create something you don't want"

We do think about a whole lot of things every day. We wake up and get ready for work. Think about our work, coworkers, bosses, our clientele, trends affecting our career, changes, duties, assignments, deadlines...we may be doing our best or may be doing just enough to get by. However, we live every day, things may work for us or against us and may affect our lives in serious ways.

The fact is, not only we can survive this current of events, but also have the ability to bring about what we really want. We need to understand what "is" should never take the hold of our hopes and dreams:

> "Many around you want to point out the "reality" to you. They say, "Face the facts. Look at what-is." And we (Abraham) say to you, if you are able to see only what-is-then, by Law of Attraction, you will create only more of what-is...You must be able to put your thoughts beyond what-is in order to attract something different or something more."

For me this is something that needed persistent practice to break through. It is indeed a common, ordinary, everyday, barrier that I had to (and still have to) overcome in order to continue my journey. I can't get enough of Abraham's advise about this and he, actually, teaches this and many other "how to" techniques in different ways and different words. If one does not influence my mind the way it should so I may take action, other ones do:

> "Let others vibrate as they vibrate and want the best for them. Never mind how they are flowing to you. You concentrate on how you're flowing. Because one who is connected to the energy stream is more powerful, more influential than a million who are not."

It's like being on a mission. Make decision to not care what others think, do, or say. Same for how every thing is or appears to be. The universe orchestrates events based on and, in fact, is responding to what we think and say; what happens, when happens, and how events happen is based on thought currents in our head and words in our mouth. If someone or something is affecting our thoughts and influencing our words; self talk and/or conversations with others, then that "one" or "thing" is creating our unwanted reality. This is when we wonder how things are happening in favor of those who we dislike for whatever reason, and we are not even aware that it is NOT them; we are doing it to ourselves.

> "You just cannot kill everybody who doesn't agree with you. You can't do it. You'll kill enough of them, and pretty soon, you'll be down to the nitty gritty that is just *you* guys, and then *you'll* start disagreeing with each other... In other words, you cannot get to where you want to be by pushing against what you do not want - it never, ever works."

Do not expect others to drop what they like because of your preferences or dislikes. Do not be envious or critical of what others gain, have, or achieve. Do not worry. No one can take more than their own share and nothing stands in your way to have what your heart desires:

> "There is a big mix out there, and there's lots of different things going on, and there is not one way that was intended to be the right way. Just like there's not one color or one flower or one vegetable or one fingerprint. There is not one that is to be the right one over all others."

I think this is not just about the variety, but the effects of it, the expansion and creation due to the "contrast" and that is why we must choose as we wish and not worry about anything else. We must understand that the adversities serve us in a way that we can't help but keep at what we desire and if we keep our focus on our wants they begin to manifest:

> "The variety is what fosters the creativity. And so you say, "Okay, I accept that there's lots of variety, but I don't like to eat cucumbers." Don't eat cucumbers. But don't ask them to be eliminated... don't ruin your life by pushing against. Instead, say, "I choose this instead. This does please me.

However, we have been limited with lots of dos and don'ts as well as rights and wrongs during the years we were growing up. Presently, I better understand where most of the difficulty in achieving one's desires has come from. Yes, there has been a time when our parents and teachers encouraged us to study, go to university, etc. but I do not believe we have ever been thought to pursue our dreams the way Abraham does:

> "Since nothing matters to you other than your personal alignment with your individual goals or desires, then that is where our work is. We are not here to debate the rightness or the wrongness of what you, or anyone chooses."

This is very much contrary to what most of us have grown up with. Almost every step of the way there has been someone to tell us "no", or "this is not right". For example, I remember my parents and I when I was in my teens, my thoughts vs theirs, and years later my thoughts and values vs my teenage daughter's. Abraham's perspective is quite different:

> "We are not taking sides, for or against, anything. We are here to help you understand that your life can be as wonderful or as horrible as you allow it to be. It all depends upon the thoughts that you practice. And therein lies the basis of anyone's success: How much do I practice thoughts that bring me joy, and

how much do I practice thoughts that
bring me pain?"

With so much emphasis on thoughts, I truly believe that
the process of thinking is the most expensive activity
that has been taken for granted and, in fact, wasted to a
grate extent. If we give all of our attention and thoughts
to our own goals and desires would there be any room
for criticizing others or being envious of what they have?

> "When you find yourself critical of the
> way anyone has attracted or is using
> money, you are pushing money away from
> yourself. But when you realize that what
> others do with money has nothing to do
> with you…"

Basically, if I mind my own business, I will not practice
thoughts that bring me pain because I have to think and
tell the better feeling story of my life:

"…your primary work is to think and speak and do what
feels good to you, then you will be in alignment not only
about the subject of money, but about every important
subject in your physical experience."

# FEAR

Weather we worry about something or afraid, we must not forget that we are "asking for it" through focusing our thoughts and energy on what we wish to avoid. Take an inventory of what you think about and say daily. Divide a sheet of paper in two parts. Throughout a typical day record your negative thoughts on one side and the positive uplifting thoughts on the other. Pay close attention to your emotions and feelings as you record your thoughts. Which side of the paper did you write more? And the energy associated with each thought; same thoughts mean the same energy and they potentiate each other. Literally. And the final product:

> "The one who fears something the most is the one who has it most activated in their vibration. And so, it is logical that they would experience it."

It's as simple as that and very well established law. In physics we have studied the law of conservation of matter and energy; which states matter and energy can neither get created nor get destroyed but they can change from

on state to another. In this case the energy associated with thoughts eventually materialize and in return what we experience create more of the same thoughts and their associated energy.

In chemistry, when Hydrogen transforms to Helium, part of Hydrogen atom converts into energy and this happens immediately when physical and chemical characteristics of the environment are in favour of such reaction, high temperature for example. However, the energy associated with thoughts do not manifest right away due to what I call "safety margin" and Abraham, calls it "buffer of time" We have a good amount of time to mend and correct our thoughts before they bring about what we don't want:

> "The buffer of time gives you the opportunity to get it right before it manifests, to take pleasure from the vision and from the moulding it into place…"

# VIBRATIONAL MATCHING/ALIGNMENT

This is what Abraham also relates so closely to "point of attraction". Are we getting what we desire? So, back to the last example, if the "negative thoughts" side of the paper is filled and we have ran out of the space writing on the flip side now and the right side has a few items only, (and this is the pattern of our thoughts everyday) what experiences are we attracting to ourselves? Are we not making ourselves a "magnet" for the most prominent and frequent negative stuff we have been thinking and complaining about by far?

> "If there is something that you desire and it is not coming to you, it always means the same thing. You are not a **vibrational match** to your own desire."

So what should we do? How do we become a vibrational match to what we want? Abraham says it all repeatedly as it is what we need to understand and practice faithfully:

> "Not only the thought you are choosing
> right now attract the next thought and the
> next…and so on –it also provides the basis
> of your alignment with your Inner Being."

Something that I never realized up until now is this:
being the "vibrational match to our desires" is also being
in "alignment with our inner being" which is actually
the "higher intelligence" or the stream of life that is
focused in our bodies. It is where holds our desires. And
it makes more sense why we are the creators of our destiny
and whatever our life has become by far, the process of
deliberate creation, whether we are aware of it or not is
constantly creating the events and directing us along the
line. We should not waste another thought. Ever,

> "As you consistently and deliberately
> think and speak more of what you do
> want and less of what do not want, you
> will find yourself more often in alignment
> with the pure, positive essence of your
> own source…"

And the best indicator that we are in alignment with our
source/desires/innerbeing is feeling happy,

> "…you've just got to line up with what you
> want, which means –be as happy as you
> can be as often as you can be there, and
> every thing else take care of itself…"

In other words, it is our point of attraction that is the indicator which tells us if we are in alignment with source or our desires or not:

> "...the way you feel is your point of attraction, and so the law of attraction is most understood when you see yourself as a magnet getting more and more of the way you feel."

# CONTRAST AND DESIRE

So what is the point for the existence of all the adversities and unwanted in the world?

> "Contrast helps you to identify desire. Desire is summoning. It's always flowing through you. You have the opportunity of opening to the harmony of the vibration of your desire or not."

I am yet to understand this fully myself, but I have seen people reaching their goal or achieving their desire even when they were going through difficult and turbulent times. One thing I noticed is these people were not getting disappointed they were just functioning from day to day without putting too much emphasis on what was not working for them or all those reasons that signified why they were not going to succeed or reach their goal. Yes, their frustrations were obvious too, but what they were not showing was *disappointment*.

> "As the desires are being summoned through you, and you go with the flow,

> you thrive, but if you use things to be your
> excuse for not going with the flow, you
> are arguing for your limitations."

And I believe the product of arguing for our limitations is definitely disappointment. This is were we will stop trying or hoping which very likely will keep us from reaching our goals unless we decide to take a different approach,

> "We want to show you how to *go with the flow*. Which means nothing more than finding vibrational harmony with your own desire, and letting the Universal Energy that your desire is summoning to it flow to it through you. It is optimum creative experience"

# THINK-IMAGIN-MANIFAST

Many times, I have been thinking about a song and the next thing I knew, either later on the same day or a few days after the radio started playing the same song several times. Especially, the songs that I like and have not heard on my favourite station for quite some time.

Many times, I have been thinking about a friend and they either called me or I got a text or email or even encountered them somewhere not too long after thinking about them.

A true story:

Several years ago, I got a contract with a local snow removal business for the winter, every year. Two years ago, the manager referred me to someone else and he continued the service, but, he too informed me that he was planning to travel and was no longer offering the service. I had to look for another provider; however, in the meantime I thought to myself, "it would be nice if I could get the former guys to help me out this winter"

A few days later, I got an email from the original snow removal manager saying that he was aware that my contract had been cancelled and he had room for two more clients if I was still looking for someone! I must say that I was very satisfied with the laws of universe because they had worked perfect!

Be ware that I had just thought about what I wanted and the song already played in my head and I saw my driveway and front yard and stairs well shovelled and clear of snow and felt the peace of mind first.

Our good friend Abraham explains it this way:

> "Achieve, first, the vibrational essence of your desire—and then, through the crack of least resistance the manifestation will be delivered... work on the essence of the feeling of freedom; work on the essence of the feeling of empowerment..."

When thinking about the first snow remover guy I was not thinking about all those reasons why he would not contact me. I had no fear or worry about it. No what if negative scenario was passing through my mind. I just went with "the flow" and it happened,

> "...work on the essence of the feeling of Well-Being... And how do you do that? *You can imagine it already having happened and pretend what it will feel like when it is that way...*"

32

For things that are very dear and important for us the situation is more sensitive and different. We all may have a fear of losing something or not reaching our desires, however, focusing of what is already working in our favour is a very good place to start. We can keep at it and take it from there,

> "Or, you can look for things in your life that are already like that and beat the drum of that until they play a higher percentage of time in the vibrational signal that you are emanating."

# ℛELATIONSHIP

Abraham' teachings have defined the laws of universe for us and made it so very simple to talk about and understand. Basically, same rules that govern attracting material wealth and money apply to getting the relationship we desire. In fact, it is the same principle that attracts "anything" into our lives:

> "...you do not choose something by looking at it and shouting yes, I would like that. You make your choices by your attention to things. In this universe that is based on attraction..."

In fact, when we give our attention to something, we are THINKING about it. There fore, choosing what we think about, which may not seem easy at first because we are constantly distracted and receive conflicting information from our environment, becomes very important.

> "...when you look at unwanted thing, your attention to it causes an activation of the vibration within you, then the law

of attraction brings more like it in to your experience."

It becomes easier with practice. What I have been doing is protecting myself of whatever thoughts that made me feel less than happy or even right down miserable. I rather focus on what I want, how I may achieve it, what solutions exist for a certain issue and carry it from there as opposed to concentrating on the problem and focusing on how I feel about it.

Whether it is our romantic partners, friends, classmates, bosses, or co-workers, our relationship(s) follow our own lead:

> "If someone cheats you, they cannot diminish your experience. They diminish their experience. You cannot be diminished by someone cheating you unless you get all upset about being cheated and push against them and use that as your excuse to disconnect from the Stream."

For clarification, by "the Stream" Abraham is referring to the stream of wellbeing. Also bare in mind that:

> "It is not your role to make others happy; it is your role to keep yourself in balance. When you pay attention to how you feel and practice self-empowering thoughts that align with who-you-rally-are..."

I would like to continue with more of Abraham's teachings which I believe look more like tips and ways of developing a much wanted relationship(s):

> **"Why Do I Want the Relationship I Want...?** Think about what you want in a relationship and why you want it. Look for those around you who are experiencing good relationships, and feel appreciation for them..."

It is not hard to do. We all have seen people who are happy in their relationships, spend great time together, or are happily married. If not, keeping with feel good thoughts in general can help us achieve alignment with what we really want to have in our life,

> "In fact one of the fastest ways to make your way to a wonderful relationship is to find any subject that consistently feels good, and focus on that even if it has nothing to do with relationships."

Remember earlier we talked about saying a "better feeling story" of our life as opposed to focusing on what is really going on? The recipe for materialization of anything we desire is the same,

> **"My Imagination Attracts All Cooperative Relationships...**You have the power to evoke from others the relationships that you desire. But

> you cannot get to a new and improved
> situation by giving your attention to the
> current situation."

By giving our attention to the better or desirable circumstances we will be tuning into the desired frequency; like being in the right place at the right time, which makes an event happen as we have imagined and desired,

> "The universe, and all physical and non-physical players in it, is responding to the vibrations that you are offering; and there is no distinction made between the vibrations that you offer as you observe, and the vibrations that you offer as you imagine..."

Truly, our imagination is one of the most powerful tools that we have ever had at our disposal and again often not taken seriously and totally neglected as we enter adulthood. In fact, one of the greatest scientists of all times, Albert Einstein talks about imagination as "the preview of life's coming attractions" which makes it easier to understand Abraham's point of view,

> "...if you will simply imagine your life as you want it to be, all cooperative components will be summoned. And even more important, all components that are summoned will cooperate. It is Law. The experience that you have with others is about what you evoke from them."

More lessons from Abraham shows us that we will not be happy in a relationship unless we are happy and feel good about ourselves before developing connection with anybody,

> **"The Law of Attraction Assembles Happy Relationships...**Asking the relationship with any other to be the basis of buoying you up is never a good idea, because the Law of Attraction cannot bring to you something different from the way you feel."

And more advice from Abraham regarding, actually, anything we may wish to have: Feeling our way to anything desirable; becoming the person we want to attract in our lives,

> "The Law of Attraction cannot bring you a well-balanced, happy person if you are not yourself already that. The Law of Attraction, no matter what you do or say, will bring to you those who predominantly match the person who you predominantly are."

What makes it challenging is our awareness of the "lack" and not being "where we want to be" at the moment and the feelings associated with that which makes the biggest difference in achieving our desires. When we have that much money in our bank account or that nice car or the job promotion or that special someone or...I can go on

and on, but the fact is, we want all of these because it translates in to "happiness" and feeling good. We want to be happy because it "feels good" but in the awareness of not having "it" at the moment feeling good becomes difficult, and what can that create in our life?

> "Everything that everyone desires is for one reason only: they believe they will feel better in the having of it. We just want you to understand that you must feel better before it can come to you.
>
> In simple terms, if you are not happy with yourself, or with your life, the attraction of a partner will only exaggerate the discord, because any action taken from a place of lack is always counterproductive."

It was hard for me to take that "feel good before it comes" approach as Abraham puts it and still is a challenge, but I do believe that we must develop the self discipline and commitment required to become proficient in it. Once this is a second nature to us, to think and feel as we desire, everything else falls into place. Effortless perfection.

> **"Should I Leave or Should I Stay...?** It is very empowering to discover that your pattern of thought do not have to follow your current situation, and therefore your current situation (on all subjects) can change...We do not recommend taking the physical action of leaving a relationship without deliberately coming

into thought alignment with he new desires that have been born out of your current relationship. And then - whether you stay in this relationship or move on to another - you can have exactly what you desire."

There are lots and lots of great tips from Abraham regarding achieving anything we desire. What is interesting is how we may use something or a condition we do not like in order to clarify and focus on what we really really care to have,

> **"Relationships I Don't Want, Clarify those I Do Want...**Whenever you know what you do not want, you always know more clearly what you do want, so in a poignant moment of awareness of another person's undesirable situation, give your undivided attention to the idea of improvement that has hatched from your interaction/observation..."

Here is something majority of people either do not know or do not believe. I believe it is very true:

> **"By Default, I Could Have Attracted Unwanted Relationships...** Many of the relationships or experiences you have attracted you would not have deliberately attracted if you had been doing it on purpose, but much of your attraction is

not done by deliberate intent, but rather
by default…"

Not too long ago, I was listening to an audio CD from
Earl Nightingale, a respected American speaker and
author aka "The Dean of Personal Development" in
which he talks about the "secret" which he reveals as we
become what we think about. Abraham thoughts are not
any different than his,

> "It is important to understand that you
> get what you think about, whether you
> want it or not. And chronic thoughts
> about unwanted things invite, or ask
> for, matching experiences. *The Law of
> Attraction* makes it so."

And another fact that I think someday will be considered
the "golden rule" not because he who set it had the gold,
but because he who follows accordingly will have the gold:

> **"The Most Important Relationship
> Is With My Source…** There is no
> relationship of greater importance to
> achieve than the relationship between
> you, in your physical body, right here
> and now, and the Soul/Source/God from
> which you have come."

I have come to truly believe that one best way of achieving
this is through relationship with oneself. If I have a great

relationship with myself then I can have the relationship I want with anything or anybody,

> "If you tend to that relationship, first and foremost, you will then, and only then, have the stable footing to proceed into other relationships. Your relationship with your own body … money … your parents, children, grandchildren, the people you work with, your government, your world … will all fall swiftly and easily into alignment once you tend to this fundamental, primary relationship first."

# $\mathcal{U}$NABLE TO THINK POSITIVE THOUGHTS?

Wanting and intensely desiring something with an awareness of not having what we desire at the moment, or holding fearful thoughts of obstacles and adversaries at the same time almost guarantees our failure of achieving our desires. Basically, it is the "attitude of resistance" as Abraham says below, and to overcome that resistance we must make the effort of doing something we like to make us feel good,

> "Do you have to change your vibration on a particular subject in order to let it in?" No, you don't. You could pet your pet and let it in. You could sit with your feet dangling in the bay, and let it in. If it is a subject that you often think of in an attitude of resistance, it is really worthwhile reaching for some thoughts that feel better."

"Your life is right now. It's not later. It's
not the time of retirement. It's not when
the lover gets here. It's not when you have
moved into the new house. It's not when
you get the better job. Your life is right
now. It will always be right now. You
might as well decide to start enjoying your
life right now, because it's not ever going
to get better than right now—until it gets
better right now!"

So, now that we have this desire and we want it so badly,
but all kinds of worries and fears of "what ifs", "if this
happens", or "if that happens" pour into our heads and we
get so swamped in so much negativity; feel good activities
or thoughts become such a challenge Abraham has a
very interesting solution. Not only that, but the rationale
makes perfect sense,

"You could launch an intention and never
think about it again, and the Universe
would yield it to you. You don't have
to clean_up your vibration relative to
anything, if you can just not think about
it any more."

I believe this is what is called "releasing" your desire after
you stated what you want in your life. However, we need
to do this on a larger scale meaning we release the desire,
stop thinking about it, along with all other thoughts
which pass through our mind repeatedly every moment,
every day, even for a short period of time,

"...that's why we teach **meditation.** It's easier to teach you to have no thought than to have pure positive thought. When you quiet your mind you stop thought; when you stop thought you stop resistance; when you stop resistance--then you are in a state of allowing."

Having said the above, lets understand very well that being aware of our feelings and emotions is the first step towards understanding of our thought process. Our thoughts create our emotions. We must stop automatic thinking and feeling and accepting those feelings, if they are bad and negative. And yes meditation is great, however, we must practice the following for better thinking habits,

"Anytime you feel negative emotion, stop and say: *Something is important here; otherwise, I would not be feeling this negative emotion. What is it that I want?* And then simply turn your attention to what you *do* want. . . ."

And, it is really up to us to stay where we are, keep thinking what can't be done or things we can't have because, presently, we are stuck with "what is" or:

"...In the moment you turn your attention to what you want, the negative attraction will stop; and in the moment the negative attraction stops, the positive attraction will begin. And—in that moment—your

feeling will change from not feeling good
to feeling good…"

This process takes time, effort, and may be faith, but once it is a well-developed habit, it is yours and no one can take it from you.

# WHAT NEXT?

Here are my favorite quotes from Abraham because I believe it defines happiness and provides the best clue for perusing what we all desire:

> "We're asking you to trust in the wellbeing. In optimism there is magic. In pessimism there is nothing."

> "In positive expectation there is thrill and success. In pessimism or awareness of what is not wanted, there is nothing... we do not ask you to look at something that is black and call it white..."

This is where most people misunderstand their present circumstances; which they want to improve, and how it relates to laws of attraction:

> "...we do not ask that you to see something that is not as you want it to be and pretend that it is. What we ask you to do is moving your gaze. Practice changing your

> perspective. Practice talking to different
> people. Practice going to new places."

As I practiced, I found it easier to choose my thoughts
and developing good attitudes about everything I did not
have or don't have as of yet. I chose to have that picture
of super beautiful modern house in front of me every day
without feeling disillusioned or disappointed for being
in my present house, thinking it is not possible for me to
own such house. In fact, I feel exactly as Abraham puts it:

> "Practice sifting through the data for the
> things that feel like you want to feel and
> using those things to cause you feel a
> familiar place… feel familiar in your joy.
> Familiar in positive expectation, familiar
> in your knowing that all is well, because
> this universe will knock itself out giving
> you evidence of that well-being …"

Lets remember that on our way to achieving our goals the
pretty pictures must be accommodated within the great
story of our success.

> "Begin telling the story of your desire, and
> then add to it the details of the positive
> aspects that you can find that match those
> desires…"

> …And then embellish your positive
> expectation by speculating with your good
> feeling wouldn't it be nice if…? examples.

You can say things like: Only good things come to me...every time you tell your better –feeling story, you will feel better and the details of your life will improve. The better it gets, the better it gets."

# HERE ARE SOME MORE WORDS OF WISDOM FOR INTERESTED MINDS:

"...Whenever you are feeling less than good, if you will stop and say, Nothing is more important than that I feel good—I want to find a reason now to feel good,..."

"By reaching for good-feeling thoughts before you go to sleep and then experiencing the benefit of the quiet mind that occurs while you sleep—and then upon awakening, immediately turning to good-feeling thoughts—you can accomplish the ultimate Pivoting experience."

*"What-If* Everything Was Always Working Out for Me. . .?

When you play the *What-If?* game, look for things that make you feel better..."

"...When you are feeling fear or discomfort as you speak, you are not speaking of the subject of money, you are speaking of the subject of not enough money. And the

difference is very important, because the first statement brings money and the second holds it away."

"...But if you continue to look at lackful *what-is* and speak of *what-is,* you will not find the improvement that you desire..."

"When you're vibrating purely, you get only what's a match to that. It's your ambivalence: "I like that but I don't like that... I like that but I don't like that..." that keeps what you like and what you don't like coming at you all the time...when you are in vibrational harmony only with what you want. Then, only what you want comes."

"Your choices of action may be limited—but your choices of thought are not."

"Be easy about it. Don't rush into things. Savor them more. Make more plans and be more deliberate and specific about the plans you are making, and in all you do, let your dominant intent be to find that which pleasures you as you imagine it. Let your desire for pleasure and your desire for feeling good be your only guiding light..."

"Illness or pain is just an extension of negative emotion. When you are no longer feeling any resistance to it, it's a non-issue."

"The emotion you feel is always about the vibrational variance between where you want to be and where you are. If you're out of balance, there are only two ways to bring yourself into alignment: Either raise your expectation to

match your desire—or lower your desire to match your expectation."

"Anything you do to overcome or prevent, causes a spotlight on the very thing you are wanting to overcome and prevent. You cannot take enough action to compensate for the Energy that you're flowing."

"True healers know that wellness is the order of the day, so they do not allow themselves, even for a moment, to see anything other than that. So, the power of the healer is in the power to influence the one who needs to be healed into a vibration that allows the healing that they are summoning. (that they *could* get, even without the healer, but they can get faster with a healer's influence)"

"No matter where I'm going, no matter what I'm doing, no matter who I'm doing it with, it is my dominant intent to look for what I'm wanting to see, to look for things that feel good," and the more you develop the habit of that kind of vibration—the more the Universe understands that that's who you are! And so, the more you have access only to those kinds of things!"

"If your desire is strong enough, it doesn't matter what your beliefs are. If you have a desire that is strong enough, that desire will be the dominant vibration, and it will over-ride any other vibration that you have."

"There is nothing for you to go back and live over, or fix, or feel regret about now. Every part of your life has unfolded just right. And so —now — knowing all that

you know from where you now stand, now what do you want? The answers are now coming forth to you. Go forth in joy, and get on with it."

"The only problem with leaving and going someplace else is that you take yourself with you. You take your vibrational habits and patterns with you."

# CITATIONS

Excerpted from the workshop in Virginia Beach, VA on Saturday, April 12th, 1997

Excerpted from the workshop on Thursday, Philadelphia, PA. May 12th, 2005 # 125

Excerpted from the workshop: Money and the Law of Attraction on August 31, 2008

Excerpted from the book "Money and the Law of Attraction: Learning to Attract Health, Wealth and Happiness" by Esther and Jerry Hicks

Excerpted from *Money and the Law of Attraction* — 3/31/09

Abraham-Hicks Wednesday, October 9, 2013

The Law of Attraction: The Basics of the Teachings of Abraham

By Esther Hicks, Jerry Hicks

Excerpted from the workshop: 6/10/97 — Portland, OR

Excerpted from the workshop in Washington, DC on May 7, 2005

Excerpted from: Rye, NY on October 12, 1997 workshop

Esther (and Abraham and Jerry) Hicks

Excerpted from San Francisco, CA – March 8th, 2003

Excerpted from the workshop in Tarrytown, NY on Saturday, May 10th, 2003 #205

abraham-hicks.com

Excerpted from the workshop in Ashland, OR on Tuesday, May 16th, 2000 #514

Excerpted from the workshop in Boca Raton, FL on Sunday, January 12th, 1997 # 7

Excerpted from the book "The Law of Attraction, The Basics of the Teachings of Abraham"

Abraham Hicks, The Vortex, page 21

Excerpted from the workshop: The Vortex on August 31, 2009

The Vortex: Where the Law of Attraction Assembles All Cooperative Relationships

Excerpted from the workshop: Los Angeles, CA on August 19, 2000

Excerpted from the book - "Money and the Law of Attraction"

Excerpted from the workshop in San Rafael, CA on Wednesday, March 4th, 1998

Ester Jerry Hicks, Money and the Law of Attraction: Learning to Attract Wealth, Health, and Happiness.

Excerpted from: Chicago, IL on November 01, 1998

Excerpted from: Chicago, IL on May 25, 2002

Excerpted from: Philadelphia, PA on April 14, 1998

Excerpted from: San Rafael, CA on August 03, 2002

Excerpted from: San Francisco, CA on July 24, 2004

Excerpted from: Philadelphia, PA on April 14, 1998

Excerpted from: San Francisco, CA on July 30, 2005

Excerpted from: Albuquerque, NM on May 09, 1999

Excerpted from: Atlanta, GA on September 13, 1997

Excerpted from: Virginia Beach, VA on April 12, 1997

Excerpted from: Albany, NY on May 18, 1998

www.ingramcontent.com/pod-product-compliance
Lightning Source LLC
Chambersburg PA
CBHW060646290526
45793CB00001B/425